# The Empire State Building

## and New York City

This book contains a superb collection of photographs which have been carefully selected to present a beautiful and artistic Photographic Tour of New York City. The Publisher wishes to acknowledge that it is the remarkable people of New York who create the city's unique character. While this collection has been able to capture in photographs a lasting remembrance of New York City, an actual tour will complete the experience.

On the following page is a glittering panorama of the New York skyline. Visible are the Chrysler, Pan Am and Empire State Buildings, while the Twin Towers of the World Trade Center loom in the background. Just barely visible is the lighted Statue of Liberty in New York Bay.

# INDEX

© 2005 KINA Italia / EuroGrafica

*Text:* Alvin P. Anderson
*Color photos:*
 Alan Shein
 Kina Italia - EuroGrafica
*B/W photos:*
 AP/Wide World Photos
 Columbia University
 Museum of the City of New York
 New York Public Library
 NYC Municipal Archives
 The New York Historical Society

Printed in Italy by KINA Italia /
EuroGrafica
Distributed by Empire State Building

# INTRODUCTION

New York City is a sparkling, many faceted jewel. A color-ful city filled with contradictions that can overwhelm the uninitiated and even confuse the seasoned resident. New York City is happy and sad; rich and poor, sophisticated and innocent; brilliant and drab; historic and sleekly mod-ern. History never has known a city which has grown to its proportions in such a short time. From its first settle-ments by the Dutch and British, and later by millions of immigrants from all parts of the world, New York City rapidly flourished to become the financial, commercial and cultural capital of the continent.

It has developed a unique lifestyle which has become known throughout the world. Frequently the New York City lifestyle is criticized, but more often it is imitated, and never it is as "at home" as it is in its birthplace. New York City is the prized jewel of America, and for all who seek

The first visit to New York by a European was made by Giovanni da Verrazano, a Florentine who discovered the entrance to New York Harbor in 1524. In 1609 Henry Hudson, an Englishman in Dutch employ, explored the harbor and the Hudson River which now bears his name. The harbor, which is considered to be one of the best in the world, was a prime factor in the city's rise to world prominence and in its continued supremacy. It ranks as one of the world's largest, and its well protected port is deep enough to accommodate the largest ships afloat.

The early history of New York City took place in the small area from the Battery to about where Wall Street now stands. The New York Stock Exchange began its rich history operating on a Wall Street green (small park) in 1792. In 1700 the first library was opened and the new city hall, which was to become Federal Hall,

New York City served as the Capital of the United States from 1789 to 1790.

On the steps of Federal Hall, George Washington was inaugurated the first President of the United States in 1789.

With the establishment of the new nation and its open immigration, what followed is one of the most remarkably profound phenomenon of modern history.

As the gate to the New World, New York City was called the melting pot of the nation. At its two immigration centers, Castle Clinton and Ellis Island more than 27 million immigrants were processed, many of whom remained in the city. Each group of immigrants brought with them a special way of life from their homeland. In their eagerness to build a new life, they sometimes toiled for endless hours at the most grueling labor. Their efforts contributed to the rapid growth of the city and their diverse backgrounds enriched the city's intricate culture. Today in New

York City, there are more people with Irish, Italian and Jewish ancestry than in Dublin, Rome or Tel Aviv.

New York City is a composite of many different sections which largely have retained the names of their original independent communities or derived their names from their geographical location. Examples of some of these include Harlem, Greenwich Village, Chinatown, the Lower East Side, and the Times Square District. Most of them have a colorful past which stretches into the present such as Little Italy on Mulberry Street. Settled by almost 4 million Italian immigrants between 1890 and 1924, the area is still distinctly Italian and it holds a week long celebration in September during the Feast of San Gennaro. In Chinatown, you will find pagoda-like telephone booths in an Oriental atmosphere containing the greatest concentration of Chinese restaurants in America.

The entire city of New York embraces a total of approximately 5,940 miles of streets. Its most celebrated thoroughfare is Broadway, which is popularly called the Great White Way, particularly in the Times Square District between 39th and 57th Streets. It is the home of American Theater and in the evening the electrifying magic of the theater district holds theater-goers and passers-by in its spell.

Among New York's most famous streets are the Bowery, Wall Street, representing the financial heart of the nation; Central Park South and West, Park Avenue, and SuttonPlace, expensive residential sections; Madison Avenue, the home of the advertising business; and Fifth Avenue, famous for its glamorous and exclusive shops.

New York is a city of superlatives with a glorious history but fortunately it is too young and diverse to be bound by traditions which might inhibit its perpetual change and growth. Within the five boroughs of New York City unfolds the continuing story of a nation of immigrants who have come to the gate of the United States to pursue their visions of the New World, seeking the freedom and opportunity which it offers. Today, instead of the melting pot, New York City is more appropriately referred to as the "salad bowl", because time has taught that while cultures and ethnic groups have mixed, each still has maintained a separate identity. It is these differences in culture which create an ever changing aura, giving one the impression of being in several or more different cities at one time.

New York City offers the widest panorama of art, museums, shopping, food and entertainment to which any present day city can lay claim. This Photographic Tour will help you to appreciate them.

Please enjoy it. NEW YORK CITY, diamond on the Hudson... it's one hell of a town!

**Legend**

- – – – State border
- ▢ Park
- Primary road
- ▢ Airport
- ·······  Tunnel
- 495  139  Route marker

Tenaly Natural Park

Bergen

New York Botanical Garden

Pelham Bay Park

Long Island Sound

Overpeck Country Golf Course

Inwood Hill Park

The Bronx

G. Washington Bridge

Teterbora Airport

Yankee Stadium

Ferry Point Park

Kings Point Park

Nas

Branch Brook Park

Central Park

La Guardia Airport

Kissena Park

Little Neck Bay

East River

Essex

NEW JERSEY

Lincoln Tunnel

Manhattan

495

Corona Park

Queens

Cunningham Park

Holland Tunnel

Forest Park

Liberty State Park

Brooklyn Bridge

Newark Liberty International Airport

3

Gallping Hill Park

1

Upper New York Bay

Park Slope

Brooklyn

Spring Creek Park

Newark Bay

NEW YORK

John F. Kennedy International Airport

Union

Richmond

Silver Lake Park

Dyker Beach Golf Couresse

Marine Park

Middlesex

Willow BrookPark

Staten Island

Great Kills Park

La Taurette Park

Coney Island Channel

Lower New York Bay

Atlantic Ocean

0 ___ 5 ml
0 ___ 5 km

1 Statue Of Liberty
2 Battery Park
3 Ellis Island
4 U.S. Customs House
5 South Street Seaport Museum
6 N.Y. Stock Exchange
7 Trinity Church
8 World Trade Center Memorial
9 City Hall
10 Chinatown
11 Little Italy
12 Foley Square
13 The Bowery
14 Soho
15 Washington Square

16 Gramercy Park
17 Little Church Around The Corner Art
18 Chrysler Building
19 United Nations
20 Grand Central Terminal
21 Met Life Building
22 Waldorf Astoria Indian
23 St. Bartholomew's Church
24 St. Patrick's Cathedral Park
25 Madison Square Garden
26 Empire State Building
27 New York Public Library
28 Times Square
29 Rockefeller Center
30 Radio City Music Hall

31 Museum Of Modern Art
32 Lincoln Center
33 New York Coliseum
34 Carriage Rides
35 Carnegie Hall
36 Plaza Hotel
37 Central Park Zoo
38 Temple Emanuel
39 American Museum Of Natural History
40 Hayden Planetarium
41 Metropolitan Museum Of Art
42 Guggenheim Museum
43 Columbia University
44 Grant's Tomb

# THE EMPIRE STATE BUILDING
# HISTORY AND FACTS

# 1 MAY 1931
## INAUGURATION

*T*he Empire State Building was inaugurated on May 1st, 1931, and its 1,250 feet of height made it **the tallest building in the world**. It immediately became a symbol of New York City and well reflected the atmosphere of the twentieth century, a time of great challenges.

# FACTS, NUMBERS AND DATES

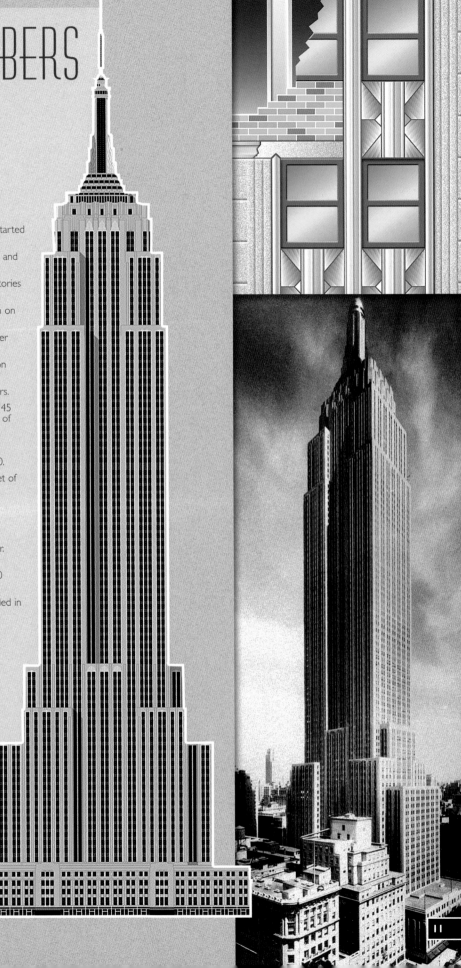

**Area of site**: 83,860 square feet.

**Demolition of the area**'s existing buildings started on January 22nd, 1930.

**Foundations** were laid on March 17th, 1930 and are 55 feet below ground.

The **steel skeleton rose** at the rate of 4,5 stories per week.

The **cornerstone** was laid by Alfred E. Smith on September 17th, 1930.

**Masonry work** was completed on November 13th, 1930.

The **official opening ceremony** took place on May 1st, 1931.

**Working time** employed: 7 million man hours.

**Construction** was completed in 1 year and 45 days of work (more than 4 months ahead of original schedule).

**Work force**: 3,400 during peak times.

**Total cost**, real estate included: $ 40,948,900.

**Cost of the buiding**: $ 24,718,000 (the onset of the Great Depression halved the initially budgeted cost).

**Floors**: 102.

**Windows**: 6,500.

**Steps**: 1,860 from street level to 102nd floor.

**Elevators**: 73, including six freight elevators; operating speeds range from 600 to 1,400 feet/minute

The **first air conditioning system** was installed in 1950.

**Total Height**:
  1,454 feet (1,453 feet, 8 9/16th inches) to top of lightning rod.

**Height**:
  - to 86th Floor Observatory: 1,050 feet.
  - to 102nd Floor Tower: 1,224 feet.
  - 102nd Floor to Tip: 230 feet.

**Height of antenna**: 204 feet.

**Total building volume**:
  37 million cubic feet.

**Weight**: 365,000 tons.

381 m
1250 ft

300 m
984 ft

319 m
1046 ft

279 m
915 ft

262 m
859 ft

259 m
850 ft

290 m
951 ft

283 m
928 ft

200 m
656 ft

0 m / ft

| Empire State Building | Chrysler Building | American International | The Trump Building | Citigroup Center | Trump World Tower | GE Building |
|---|---|---|---|---|---|---|
| 1931 | 1930 | 1932 | 1930 | 1977 | 2001 | 1933 |

▲ Eiffel Tower

▲ Woolworth Building

▲ Metropolitan Life Tower

*T*he building of the Eiffel Tower in Paris - 1889 - somehow encouraged American architects to project and build taller constructions.
The beginning of the century in New York witnessed the construction of many

skyscrapers: the Metropolitan Life Tower in 1909 - 50 stories, 700 feet -, the Woolworth Building in 1913 - 57 stories, 792 feet- and the Bank of Manhattan Building in 1929 - 71 stories, 927 feet - were milestones and astonishing examples of this architectural

"nouvelle vague". By the end of 1929 New York could count a total of 188 skyscrapers.
The American Great Depression (October 29th, 1929 - 1930's) then broke out and most construction projects involving the building of skyscrapers came to a stop.

# WALDORF ASTORIA HOTEL

*W*hen John Jacob Raskob (former Vice President of General Motors) decided to join in the race, Walter Chrysler (founder of the Chrysler Corporation) was financing the construction of a skyscraper, the height of which he was keeping secret. In 1929, Raskob and his partners bought some property at 34th Street and Fifth Avenue; the area included the glamorous **Waldorf Astoria Hotel**. The Hotel was sold to Bethlehem Engineering Corporation in 1928, for an estimated $20 million.

In 1929, the Empire State, Inc. was formed and the property purchased from the Bethlehem Engineering Corporation.

Before the foundation of bedrock could be placed, the old Waldorf Astoria Hotel had to be torn down; approximately 2,000 tons of iron, 13,000 tons of steel, and tons of other material had to be removed and taken apart. What could not be sold or saved was dumped into the ocean at about 15 miles from Sandy Hook, New Jersey. The hotel was completely demolished by the end of January, 1930.

# THE PROJECT

*S*hreve, Lamb & Harmon were chosen to be the architects for what was intended to become the highest building in the world.
The task was indeed "quite simple", as J. J. Raskob presented his idea to William Lamb asking him, « Bill, how high can you make it so that it won't fall down? »

**The architectural reasoning and logic of the plan were very simple**. *Central space had to be arranged as compactly as possible, therefore including all the vertical circulation, toilets, shafts and corridors, while the surrounding perimeter had to be dedicated to office space. Floor dedicated areas decreased as the elevators increased in number.*

*The race (no one really knew how high the Chrysler skyscraper would have gone) was becoming fiercely competitive. With the thought of wanting to make the Empire State Building higher, Raskob himself came up with the solution. After examining a scale model of the proposed building, Raskob said, "It needs a hat!", such hat to be used as a docking station for dirigibles. The new design for the Empire State Building, including the dirigible mooring mast, would make the building 1,250 tall (once completed, the Chrysler Building was 1,046 feet high and had 77 stories).*

# BUILDING THE EMPIRE STATE
## CHOOSING THE CONTRACTOR

J. J. **Raskob** interviewed numerous contractors with specific expertise in the field of building skyscrapers, but the story on how **Starrett Bros. & Eken** were chosen is quite peculiar. First of all, builders Starrett Bros. & Eken assured Raskob that only eighteen months were needed for completion of the project. Secondly, when asked during the interview how much equipment they had on hand, Mr. Starrett surprised the audience by honestly stating that they had none. His reasoning for such answer proved to be the winning point: due to the unusual problems connected with the erection of such a monster, ordinary building equipment would have been unfit for such a job, and consequently needed to be replaced by custom made equipment. He then explained that such approach would have been cost beneficial; his honesty and clever approach led Raskob to choose Starrett's company for the bid.

*A*dmiring the numerous skyscrapers in New York can be considered a journey and a cultural experience through the **different architectural styles of the 20th Century**.

The **Woolworth Building** is probably the best example for skyscrapers of "Beaux Arts"; the revisiting of past styles - such as Classic, Gothic and Renaissance - was embraced by great Architects such as Gilbert, Meade and White, McKim.

While the crown of the Chrysler Building is considered an absolute Art Déco masterpiece, the **Empire State Building**'s enormous stainless steel pylons are spectacular examples of the Bauhaus culture.

The design of the Empire State Building, conceived and developed by William Lamb, finds its heartly inner strength in the two-hundred and ten steel columns forming the vertical frame. Lamb was strongly influenced, as he openly admitted, by the vertical style expression of another Architect, Elie Saarinen.

The perpendicular design of the ESB easily finds its brilliance given by the chrome-nickel steel rails, reinforcing the tower's verticality. Some architecture critics commented at the time of construction that the floral design caps at the tops of the mullions were out of character, but they are minimal and their impact marginal.

The communications antenna installed 30 years after the building's completion improved the building's silhouette by sharpening its peak.

Stone cladding of Indiana limestone and granite, trimmed with aluminum and chrome-nickel steel, were the materials used on the exterior from the 6th floor to the top of the building. For the interior - the lobby ceiling, the elevators and the office floor corridors - marble, imported from France, Italy, Belgium and Germany, was used.

# TECTURE IN NEW YORK
## AN INDISSOLUBLE TIE

The essential design and pure lines of the so called "International Style" find their best examples in the **United Nations Headquarters** and the **Met-Life** scryscraper; the projects of Le Corbusier and Mies van der Rohe well represent this style (1930/1970).

Post-modernism architecture is exemplified by the **Trump Tower**; individualism and the melting of different past styles are the remarkable leading signs of such style.

17

# KING KONG MOVIES

*P*erhaps the most famous popular culture representation of the building is in the 1933 film *"King Kong"*, in which the title character, a giant ape, climbs to the top to escape his captors, and eventually dies by falling off of it. In 1983, for the 50th anniversary of the film, an inflatable King Kong was placed on the real Empire State Building. However, a mouse chewed through it one day, partially deflating the ape. He also needed a constant supply of air, and was never fully inflated.

The observation deck was the designated site for romantic rendezvous in the films *"Love Affair"* and *"Sleepless In Seattle"* and a phony Martian invasion in an episode of *"I Love Lucy"*.

An episode of the puppet science fiction series *"Thunderbirds"* involves an attempt to move the building on tracks to a new location.

In the movie *"Independence Day"*, the building is destroyed by a gigantic alien ship.

▼ I love Lucy, 1954

18

# ELEVATORS

*H*ave you ever stood waiting in a ten story building for an elevator that seemed to take forever? Or have you ever gotten into an elevator and it took forever to get to your floor because the elevator had to stop at every floor to let someone on or off? The Empire State Building was going to have 102 floors and expected to have 15,000 people in the building. How would people get to the top floors without waiting hours for the elevator or climbing the stairs? To help with this problem, the architects created **seven banks of elevators**, with each servicing a portion of the floors. For instance, Bank A serviced the third through seventh floors while Bank B serviced the seventh through 18th floors. This way, if you needed to get to the 65th floor, for example, you could take an elevator from Bank F and only have possible stops from the 55th floor to the 67th floor, rather than from the first floor to the 102nd.

***Making the elevators faster was another solution.*** The Otis Elevator Company installed 58 passenger elevators and eight service elevators in the Empire State Building. Though these elevators could travel up to 1,200 feet per minute, the building code restricted the speed to only 700 feet per minute based on older models of elevators. The builders took a chance, installed the faster (and more expensive) elevators (running them at the slower speed) and hoped that the building code would soon change. A month after the Empire State Building was opened, the building code was changed to 1,200 feet per minute and the elevators in the Empire State Building were speeded up.

# A PORT IN THE SKY

*A*l Smith, one of the ESB main sponsors, was convinced that the building could have been **a perfect dirigible port**; for this reason, and in spite of the engineers' doubts, a mooring station was built where the base of the television tower is now positioned, on the 102$^{nd}$ floor.

Passengers could have flown directly into the heart of Manhattan, therefore avoiding the inconvenience of landing somewhere far from the City; a great save of time!

Nevertheless, only once did a dirigible dock at the mast. In September 1931, a small, privately owned dirigible made contact with the top of the Empire State Building. Dropping a long rope, a ground crew of three were able to catch the rope and hold onto it. Though it took the small dirigible over half an hour to accomplish this, it was only able to stay moored for three minutes.

Strong and unpredictable winds, and the need for passengers to embark and disembark on a catwalk 1,350 feet above the ground soon convinced Al Smith to abandon the project.

# THE B-25 THAT CRASHED INTO THE ESB

*O*n the morning of Saturday, **July 28th, 1945**, at 9:49 AM, a U.S. Army B-25 bomber crashed into the north side of the Empire State Building.

Because of the foggy weather conditions, the plane piloted by Lt. Colonel W. Smith hit the 79th floor into the offices of the "War Relief Services of the National Catholic Welfare Conference": the subsequent explosion expanded its flames all the way down to the 75th floor.

One of the engines of the airplane devastated the entire floor to find its way out of the south wall's windows, falling at last on a twelve-story building on 33rd street.

Eleven of the office workers were burned to death, whereas the total death toll counted 14 victims (the office workers and the three members of the B-25 crew); 26 other people were severely injured.

The integrity of the Empire State Building was not affected, while damages amounted to a total of $ 1 million.

When public heard that the Waldorf Astoria Hotel and the surrounding area were going to be demolished, **a man from Iowa** offered to buy the Fifth Avenue side iron railing fence.

When workers completed the steel skeleton, a **massive cheer** rose up with hats waiving. The last rivet, made of solid gold, was given the honor of a specific ceremony.

According to a study of the National Park Service, the Empire State Building is visited each year by **more than 4 million tourists**, coming from all U.S. States and from almost every country in the world.

Most of the office space could not be leased when the Empire State Building was first completed; this is why it also became known as the "**Empty State Building**".

In 1955 the American Society of Civil Engineers named the Empire State Building one of the "**Seven Modern Wonders** of the Western Hemisphere".

February 7th, 2001: the 24-year-old Australian Paul Crake wins the 24th **Annual Fleet Empire State Building Run-up** covering the building's 1,576 stairs in nine minutes and 37 seconds, therefore setting the record which is still unbeaten.
The oldest runner is a 89-year-old man from Italy who accomplished the task in 35 minutes and five seconds.

**May 1st, 2001** - The ESB is illuminated in white lights as it was on inauguration day, May 1st, 1931.

June, 2001 - The American Society of Civil Engineers granted several structures with the title of "**Monuments of the Millennium**". Included on the list are the Panama Canal, the Empire State Building, and the Golden Gate Bridge.

**11 September, 2001** - After the terroristic attack on the "Twin Towers" the Empire State Building becomes once again the tallest building in New York City.

# THE UNDISPUTED PROTAGONIST

OF NEW YORK'S SKYLINE

# COLORS OF ESB

*T*he Empire State Building is famous for **the illumination of its top thirty stories**. *It's not neon operated as buildings in Dallas or Houston, but more simply accomplished using just basic floodlights. The first special-purpose illumination on the Empire State Building was a simple searchlight. It was used to celebrate Franklin Delano Roosevelt, former Governor of New York State, who had won the presidential race in 1932.*

*The single light was substituted in 1956 by a system of four rotating searchlights known as the "Freedom Lights", symbolically welcoming people to America. In 1964 the top 30 floors of the building were all illuminated in white for the World's Fair, using fixed lamps. In 1976 red, white, and blue lights celebrated the nation's bicentennial.*

*Blue and white were used when the Yankees won baseball's World Series in 1977.*

*In spring and in autumn, when birds migrate, lights are turned off to avoid disturbing the birds on their route.*

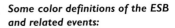

## Some color definitions of the ESB and related events:

**No Light**
AIDS Awareness
National Day of Mourning

**Black/Green/Gold**
Jamaica Independence

**Blue**
Child Abuse Prevention
Colon Cancer Awareness
Muscular Dystrophy
National Kids' Day / Boys & Girls Clubs
Police Memorial Day
Police Memorial Week

**Blue/Blue/Green**
Anniv. of National Council of Jewish Women

**Blue/Blue/White**
100th Anniversary, College of New Rochelle
Anniversary of Academy of American Poets
Anniversary of Children's Aid Society

**Blue/White/Blue**
Americans with Disabilities
Israel Independence Day

**Blue/White/Red**
Bastille Day

**Blue/White/White**
United Nations Day

**Green**
St. Patrick's Day

**Green/White/Red**
Anniversary of Mexico's Independence

**Green/Yellow/Blue**
Brazil Independence

**Orange/Blue/Blue**
NY Knicks Opening Day

**Orange/Orange/White**
Netherlands' Queens Day
Walk to End Domestic Violence

**Orange/White/Green**
India Independence

**Pink/Pink/White**
Breast Cancer Research Foundation

**Purple/Purple/White**
Alzheimer's Awareness

**Red**
Multiple Sclerosis Society
St. Valentine's Day

**Red/Black/Green**
Dr. Martin Luther King, Jr. Day

**Red/Black/Green**
30th Anniversary of HARLEM WEEK

**Red/Blue/White**
New York Rangers

**Red/Red/Green**
Holiday Colors

**Red/Red/Yellow**
Anniversary of US Marines

**Red/White/Blue**
Armed Forces Day
Flag Day
Memorial Day
Independence Day
Labor Day
Lincoln's Birthday
Veterans Day

**Red/White/Green**
Columbus Day

**Red/Yellow/Green**
Portuguese Independence

**White**
ESB Lighting

**Yellow**
U.S. Tennis Open

# VIEWS
## FROM THE EMPIRE STATE BLDG.

**500 Fifth Avenue**
*NW corner, 42nd Street*
59 stories, 1930

**Sony (AT&T)**
*550 Madison Av, 55th to 56th Sts*
37 stories, 1984

**Chase World Headquarters**
*270 Park 47-48 Sts*
53 stories, 1960

**Citigroup Center**
*Lexington Av at 53rd St*
59 stories, 1978

**General Motors Bldg**
*5th to Madison Avs,
58th to 59th St*
50 stories, 1968

**Tower 49**
*12 East 49th Street,
between 5th & Madison Avs*
45 stories, 1984

**Bear Stearns**
*383 Madison Av,
46th-47th Sts*
45 stories, 2002

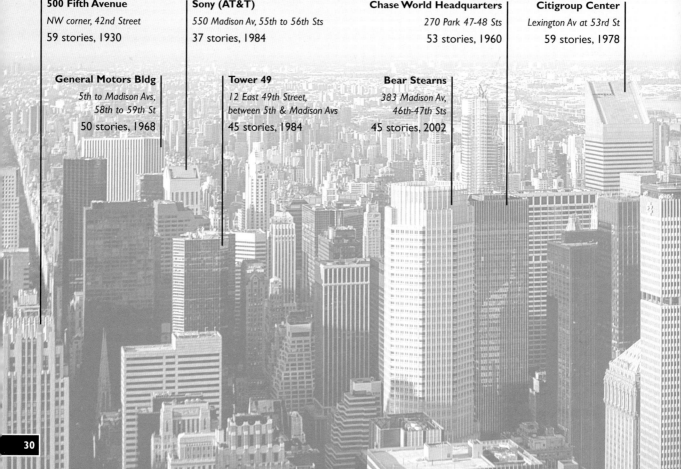

**Met Life Building
(originally Pan Am)**
*Park Avenue at 44th St*
58 stories, 1961

**450 Lexington**
*at 45th St*
40 stories, 1992

**Chrysler Building**
*Lexington Av at 42nd St*
77 stories, 1930

**Queensboro Bridge**
*59th Street Bridge*
1909

**Lincoln Building**
*60 East 42nd St*
55 stories, 1930

**Graybar Building**
*Lexington Av at 43rd St*
31 stories, 1927

**Kalikow Bldg**
*101 Park Av at 40th St*
1909

**Trump World Tower**
*47th St & First Av Costas Kondylis*
72 stories, 2001

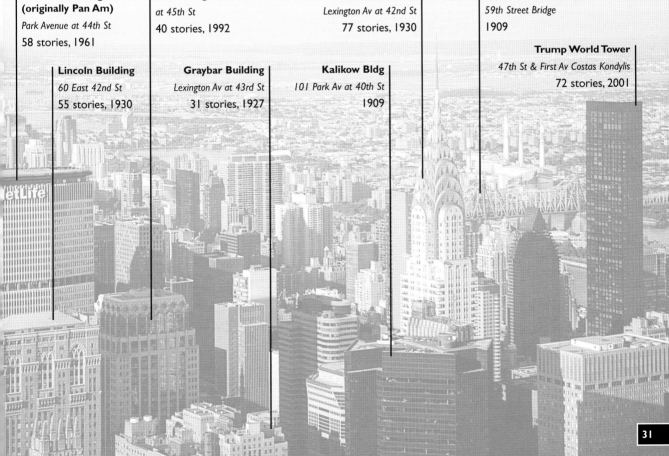

**Trump World Tower**
*47th St & First Av*
72 stories, 2001

**New York Helmsley Hotel**
*600 Third Av at 39th St*
42 stories, 1972

**UN Secretariat**
*First Av at 43rd St*
39 stories, 1952

**Paramount Tower Apts.**
*240 E 39th St, bet 2nd & 3rd Avs*
52 stories, 1999

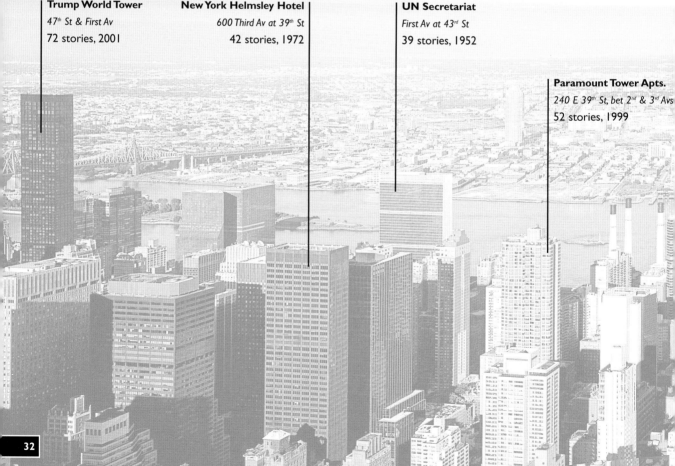

**Rivergate Apartments**
*First Av 34th to 35th Sts*
35 stories, 1985

**Waterside Apartments**
*East of FDR Drive, 25th to 30th Sts*
37 stories, 1974

**Corinthian Apts First Av**
*between 37th & 38th streets*
57 stories, 1988

**3 Park Avenue**
*33rd to 34th Sts*
42 stories, 1976

**Bellevue Medical Center**
*First Av to FDR Drive 30th to 34th*
1950

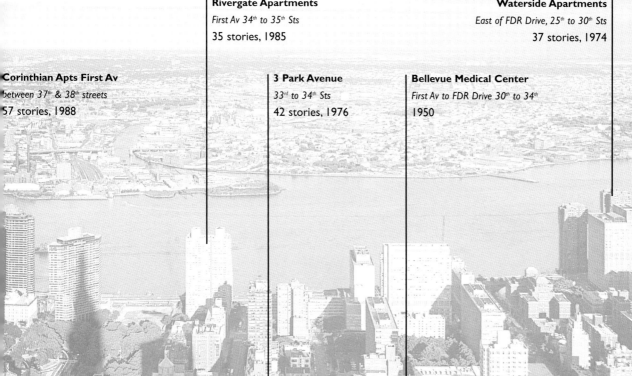

**Manhattan Bridge**

**New York Life Insurance Company**
*Madison to Park Avs, 26th to 27th*
33 stories, 1928

**Metropolitan Life Tow⬤**
*Madison Av at 24th*
52 stories, 190⬤

**Brooklyn Bridge**
1883

**Merchandise Mart**
*Madison Av SE corner, 26th St*
42 stories, 1972

**Lower Manhattan**

**Statue of Liberty**

**Flatiron Building**
*Madison Av at 24th St*
21 stories, 1902

**Fifth Avenue**

**Astor Plaza**
*44th to 45th Sts*
54 stories, 1972

**Verizon**
*Sixth Avenue at 41th St*
1970

**Grace Building**
*1114 Sixth Avenue*
50 stories, 1973

**Central Park**

**St. Patrick Cathedral**
*500 Fifth Avenue at 42nd St*
59 stories, 1930

| Ludlow & Peabody | Lincoln Buiding | Met Life Building | Chrysler Building | Kalikow Bldg |
|---|---|---|---|---|
| *40th St to 39th St* | *60 East 42nd St* | *Park Avenue at 44th St* | *Lexington Av at 42nd St* | *101 Park Av at 40th St* |
| 48 stories, 1929 | 55 stories, 1930 | 58 stories, 1961 | 77 stories, 1930 | 49 stories, 1982 |

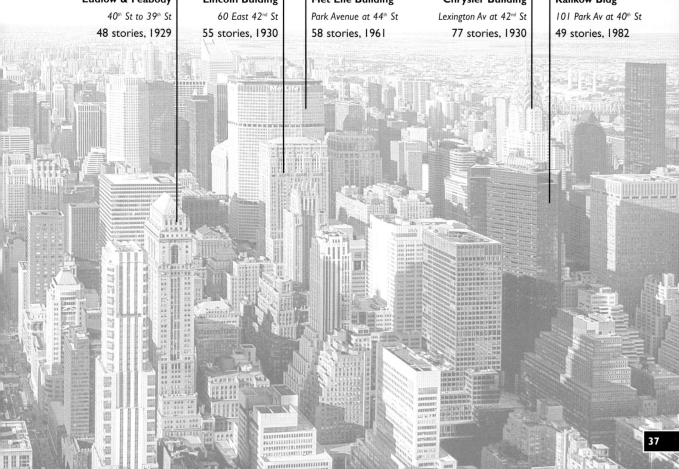

# NEW YORK TOUR

# TIMES SQUARE

*T*he intersection of **Broadway** and 42<sup>nd</sup> Street is also known as "***Crossroads of the World***". The Broadway scene offers a wide pot-pourri of theaters, movie theaters, restaurants, shops and bars.

*F*irst Avenue between E. 42ⁿᵈ and E. 48ᵗʰ Sts. This 18 acre site is dominated by the 39-story glass and marble **Secretariat**, while the General Assembly Building has low sweeping lines. The Conference Building and its world-famous **Security Council Chamber**, together with the Hammarskjold Library, complete the site. The large lobby of the General Assembly is the visitors' entrance to the Headquarters. The land on which the United Nations complex was built was acquired as a result of combined donations of John D. Rockefeller, Jr. and the City of New York. The four main buildings were erected in 1950 under the direction of Architect Wallace K. Harrison at a cost of approximately $ 67,000,000.

The low-lying structure on the riverside is the **"Conference Building"** where the Economic and Social, the Trusteeship, and the Security Councils hold their sessions. The three chambers are of identical dimensions, 72-feet wide, 135-feet long, and with 24-feet ceilings.

View opposite the East River: the United Nations (left end side) and the skyscrapers of midtown Manhattan.

# CENTRAL PARK

*L*aunched by William Cullen Bryant, designed by Calvert Vaux and Frederick Law Olmstead in the 1840's, Central Park provides New Yorkers with a country setting surrounded by stainless steel superstructures. The Park sponsors and promotes **many events**, including concerts, festivals and contests. It's the only U.S. municipal park officially given the national landmark status. North to south, it extends for 2 miles from 59th to 110th Streets, and for half a mile across town, from Central Park West to Fifth Avenue.

# WITHIN CENTRAL PARK

Within the 840 acres of the park are the **Central Park Zoo**, **Wollman Memorial Skating Ring**, the **Metropolitan Museum of Art** and other cultural and sports facilities.

The **Plaza Hotel** is the epitome of luxury and elegance. Built in 1907, it is the gathering place for royalty, New York Society and visiting dignitaries. It is located at 59th Street and Fifth Avenue, next to the Grand Army Plaza where the equestrian statue of General Sherman and the Winged Victory are.

The **Coliseum** and **Columbus Circle** located at 59ᵗʰ Street and 8ᵗʰ Avenue. It is the scene of important trade shows, numerous conventions and expositions. ▼

▲ Horse-drawn carriages are available at the southeast corner of Central Park for a leisurely ride.

# THE METROPOLITAN MUSEUM OF ART

# LINCOLN CENTER

*B*roadway and 65ᵗʰ *Street. Designed and built in the 1960s, the complex includes Avery Fisher Hall, New York State Theater, Metropolitan Opera House, Library and Museum of the Performing Arts, Vivian Beaumont Theater, the Juilliard School, Alice Tully Hall and the Guggenheim Bandshell in Damrosch Park.*

*The complex combines **artistic and educational institutions**, making it one of the most distinctive cultural centers in the world. Opera, ballets, concerts, plays and other activities are performed at the same time.*

*L*incoln Center Plaza is an exciting location to stroll; outdoor dining during warmer months is a truly unique experience.

The top photograph, from left to right, gives a view of the New York State Theater, the Metropolitan Opera House, and the Avery Fisher Hall. The bronze in the reflecting pool, "**Reclining Figure**", is located on the North Plaza, in front of the Vivian Beaumont Theater.

# ROCKEFELLER CENTER

*F*ifth Avenue - **Avenue of the Americas**, 47ᵗʰ - 52ⁿᵈ Sts. Development of the area begun in the early 1930's, but this 24-acre office buildings complex is still expanding. An extensive underground concourse offers a wide variety of shops and restaurants. The Channel Gardens feature spectacular seasonal floral displays among fountains and shallow pools. The 18-foot-high **sculpture of Prometheus**, a work of Paul Manship, is cast in bronze and covered with gold leaves.

◄ At 5ᵗʰ Avenue and 50ᵗʰ St., the 45 foot-high statue of Atlas; the seven-ton bronze statue by Lee Lawrie was installed in 1937; on the bottom, ice skating in winter on the Lower Plaza.

# RADIO CITY MUSIC HALL

*A*venue of the Americas and 50th St. Inaugurated in 1932, it is **the world's biggest indoor theater**, with a seating capacity of 6,200 people. Radio City introduced theater lovers to the famed Rockettes, the world's finest precision dancers. Designed in Art Déco style, this building is also renowned for its richly decorated interiors.

# CHURCHES

◀ **Temple Emanuel**, *Fifth Avenue and 65ᵗʰ St. Completed in 1929, this Romanesque style construction houses a Reform Congregation founded in 1845.*

▼ *The 330 foot-high twin spires of* **St. Patrick's Cathedral**. *Erection of the Gothic style Cathedral, designed by James Renwick, begun in 1858; St. Patrick was consecrated in 1910.*

**Cathedral of St. John the Divine**, *Amsterdam Avenue at 122ᵗʰ St. Under construction for more than half a century, originally conceived in Romanesque style, the Cathedral was later changed to French Gothic.*

**Little Church around the corner**, *29ᵗʰ St., East of Fith Avenue. The Protestant Episcopal Church of the Transfiguration is a favorite of theater loving people.*

# STATUE OF LIBERTY

The 152-foot statue is constructed of hand-hammered copper plate and stands upon a granite pedestal. Created by sculptor Frederic A. Bartholdi, it utilizes an iron framework designed by Gustave Eiffel. The statue was donated to the United States by France in 1886 to commemorate the alliance between France and the U.S.A.; the book in the left hand represents the Declaration of Independence. The 10 by 17 foot chamber on her head offers a superb view of the City.

The statue is located on **Liberty Island in Upper New York Bay**; the island lies partly in the States of New York and New Jersey. It can be easily reached by ferry boat from the Battery.

The Statue of Liberty has lifted her **welcoming torch in New York Harbor** for over 100 years. Painstakingly constructed by craftsmen in France and then shipped to the United States in pieces, it was then installed by Americans. The Statue has just recently undergone extensive renovation and re-opened to visitors in the summer of 2004.

Within view of the Statue are **Ellis Island** and **Battery Park**. Ellis Island was the place of entry for millions of immigrants to America, while Battery Park's **Castle Clinton** is strategically located to guard the harbor.

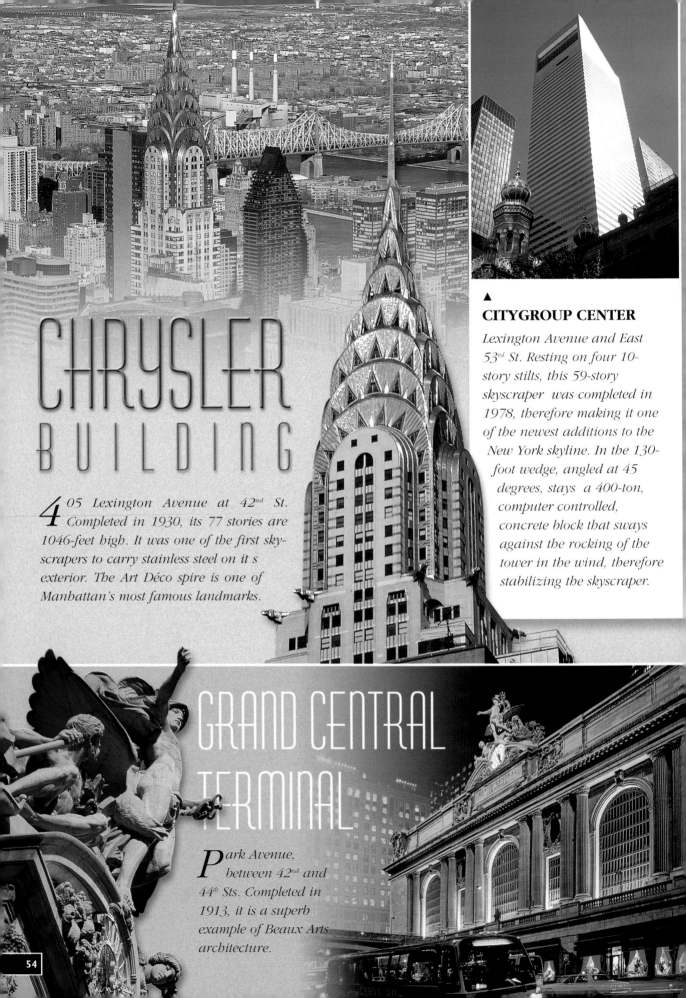

# CHRYSLER BUILDING

4 05 Lexington Avenue at 42ⁿᵈ St. Completed in 1930, its 77 stories are 1046-feet high. It was one of the first skyscrapers to carry stainless steel on it s exterior. The Art Déco spire is one of Manhattan's most famous landmarks.

## ▲ CITYGROUP CENTER

Lexington Avenue and East 53ʳᵈ St. Resting on four 10-story stilts, this 59-story skyscraper was completed in 1978, therefore making it one of the newest additions to the New York skyline. In the 130-foot wedge, angled at 45 degrees, stays a 400-ton, computer controlled, concrete block that sways against the rocking of the tower in the wind, therefore stabilizing the skyscraper.

# GRAND CENTRAL TERMINAL

P ark Avenue, between 42ⁿᵈ and 44ᵗʰ Sts. Completed in 1913, it is a superb example of Beaux Arts architecture.

### ▲ FIFTH AVENUE

*One of the greatest places in the world to stroll and shop, this avenue captures the excitement and glamour of New York.*

### ▲ PARK AVENUE

*This famous street well describes the elegance, luxury and wealth of New York. St. Bartholomew's Church is on the left of the photograph.*

### ▲ METLIFE BUILDING

*(Originally PAN AM). Park Avenue between 44th and 45th Sts. One of the largest office buildings in the world; more than 25,000 people are employed here.*

# GUGGENHEIM MUSEUM

*Fifth Avenue and 89th Street. It is the only New York structure designed by Frank Lloyd Wright. Its collection of abstract, avant-garde, and contemporary art is exhibited using a circular ramp.*

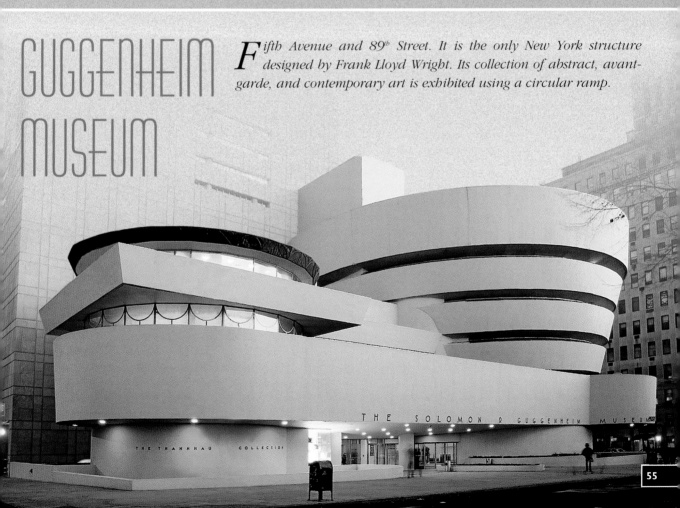

THE THANNHAU    COLLECTION

THE SOLOMON R GUGGENHEIM MUSEUM

*T*he **Brooklyn Bridge**, the first bridge to span the East River to Brooklyn was first open to traffic in 1883; toll was one penny. The second structure crossing the East River to Brooklyn was the **Williamsburg Bridge**.

**Manhattan Bridge** is located in the center; its decorations are reminiscent of Paris Eiffel Tower.

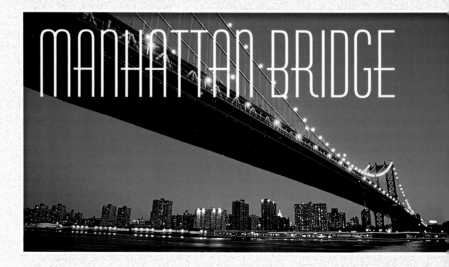

MANHATTAN BRIDGE

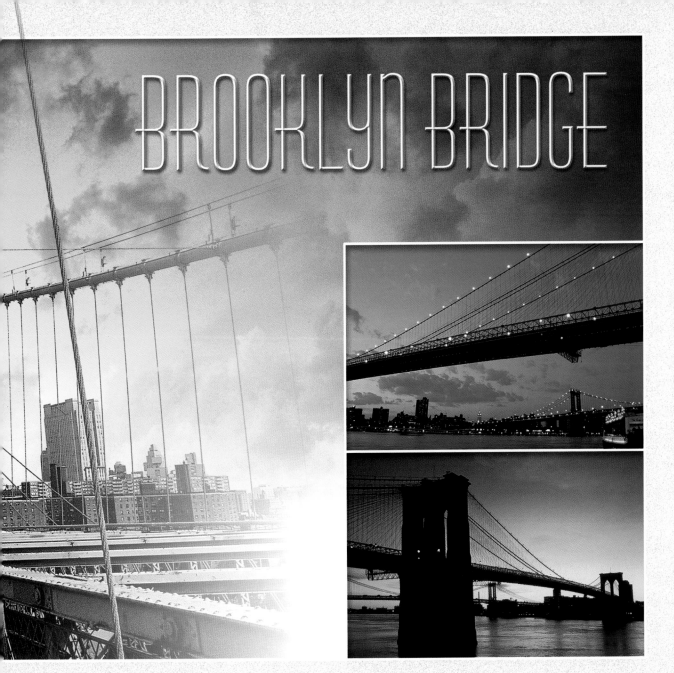

# BROOKLYN BRIDGE

▲

## GEORGE WASHINGTON BRIDGE

*The two-level George Washington Bridge crosses the Hudson River between upper Manhattan (West 178th Street) and Fort Lee, New Jersey, and forms part of Interstate Highway I-95.*

▲

## QUEENSBORO BRIDGE

*Built in 1909, the bridge connects Long Island City with Manhattan at 59th Street.*

# GREENWICH VILLAGE

*I*t is **the gathering place for artists, intellectuals, students** *and people of all kinds. The park, surrounded by New York University, maintains a carnival atmosphere year-round. Street entertainers take over the center fountain to amuse the dog walkers, skateboarders, musicians and chess players who make full use of the park. Although much of the fabled Beatnik-era ambiance is gone, you'll find coffeehouses like Caffe Reggio and Cafe Figaro which inspired writers such as Jack Kerouac and William Burroughs.*

## AVENUE OF THE AMERICAS

*Running from the Greenwich Village to 59th Street, it is one of the City's leading commercial areas and home of numerous major Corporations.*

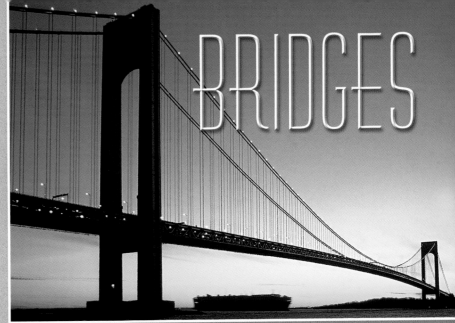

# BRIDGES

▲

## VERRAZANO NARROWS BRIDGE

*When it opened in 1964, the Verrazano Narrows Bridge was the world's longest suspension span. Today, its length is surpassed only by the Humber Bridge in England. The bridge connects Brooklyn and Staten Island.*

# LITTLE ITALY

*Little Italy is a neighborhood in southern Manhattan, New York City, once known for its population of Italian immigrants. The Feast of San Gennaro is a large street fair, lasting 11 days, that takes place every September along Mulberry Street between Houston Street and Canal Street.*

# CHINATOWN

*Squeezed into a tiny area of lower Manhattan, Chinatown has remained an immigrant enclave and retained **its unique cultural personality**. Starting on Canal Street, business pours out of storefronts and onto the sidewalk where the art of bargaining is always handy.*

# MANHATTAN ISLAND

▼ A spectacular and extraordinary aerial photograph, from the Battery to the Bronx.

▲ *Castle Clinton*, *was strategically located to guard the harbor. In later years, it was renamed Castle Garden and served as the country's immigration station from 1855 to 1890.*

▲ *Battery Park on the southern tip of Manhattan, where the City of New York had its beginning. Located on 21 open acres looking out to sea.*

**NY STOCK EXCHANGE AND WALL STREET**

AMERICAN STOCK EXCHANGE

# SOUTH STREET SEAPORT

*South Street Seaport preserves **New York's seaport heritage**. A restored row of Federal houses, tall-masted ships, new restaurants, shops and galleries provide an exciting and informative place for any visitor.*

The World Trade Center was originally proposed to be built at the Fulton Fish Market on the East River, but it was later decided to relocate the project to Lower Manhattan's west side.

Architect Minoru Yamasaki was selected to design the project; the WTC had its ribbon-cutting ceremony on April 4, 1973. Ultimately the complex came to consist of 7 buildings, but its most notable features were the main twin towers.

Each of the WTC towers had 110 stories. To solve the problem of wind sway or vibration, each tower innovatively contained 240 vertical steel columns around the outside of the building. The heights of the towers were 1368 ft (the North Tower with a huge antenna on top) and 1362 ft (the South Tower with the observation deck).

When the towers were completed in 1972 (tower one) and 1973 (tower two) they were the tallest buildings on earth, approximately 100 ft taller than the Empire State Building.

On February 26, 1993, a bomb placed by terrorists exploded in the underground garage of the north tower; six people were killed and over a thousand injured.

On September 11, 2001, American Airlines Flight 11 crashed into the north side of the north tower of the WTC at 8:46:40 AM local time. At 9:03:11 AM local time, United Airlines Flight 175 crashed into the south tower; total casualties were close to 3,000 - including 343 NYC firefighters.

# WORLD TRADE CENTER

# MADISON SQUARE GARDEN

▲ Shea Stadium, home of the NY Mets.

▲ Hemisphere from World's Fair.

# SPORT'S TEMPLES

*N*ew York's tradition in hosting sports is a worldwide trademark. There are many stadiums, athletic fields, golf courses, race tracks and other recreational facilities.

Four of the most famous sport sites are **Shea Stadium**, home of the NY Mets - baseball -, the **Madison Square Garden**, home of the NY Knicks - basketball - and NY Rangers - ice hockey -, **Yankee Stadium**, home of the NY Yankees - baseball -, and the **New York Sports & Convention Center**, home of the NY Jets - football -.